How to be successful in affiliate marketing.
The methods and skills you need to become
successful are all in this book. All you need to do is
to read it and follow the steps.

By:
Paul Marles

What Is Affiliate Marketing?
Affiliate advertising is a cycle in which an associate will increase a enterprise' objects and administrations and receives a fee at the off hazard that the associate accomplishes a deal.

An associate is a person that makes use of its agencies and net advertising capacities to increase objects and administrations.

Affiliate advertising and the usage of associate advertisers is a offers and execution primarily based totally selling method that gives many blessings to each the enterprise and the advertiser.

While an object is brilliant, and the advertisers' net advertising skills match, each will accomplish better offers and logo mindfulness.

Affiliate advertising is a treasured method for any enterprise that desires to expand. It's offers without spending on a standard publicizing monetary plan.

Developing your associate advertising method is a protracted cycle that consists of human beings and giving them the proper devices and impetuses to increase your picture and objects.

Most usually, agencies and advertisers use associate advertising withinside the internet primarily based totally on the advertising world.

It can likewise contain the dedication of disconnected and real offers assuming that's what the company wants.

Business spending on associate advertising is growing quickly, and spending is classified to develop up to $8.2 Billion each 2022, an improvement of ~52% from 2017.

On the off-chance that your enterprise isn't always similar to the improvement of associate advertising, your power is dropping on massive internet-primarily based totally land this is simply possible the use of associate advertisers.

In this article, we can show the blessings of associate advertising advantages for agencies and moreover how associate institutions assist every celebration engaged with the cycle.

The joint blessings to the 2 gamers make associate advertising an essential piece of any superior advertising method.

On the whole, we must see how associate advertising functions.

The Ultimate Guide to Affiliate Marketing

In the case which you're investigating diverse forms of advertising in your picture, associate advertising is one method you must n't forget. Be that because it might also additionally, withinside the occasion that associate advertising seems to be extremely foggy or untested to you, it shouldn't. Manufacturers going from Levis Strauss and Co. to Hotels.com use to reach consumers on a extensive or uniqueness scale consistently. Likewise a sincerely sincere concept's been round in diverse systems for pretty a at the same time as, which helps you to realize that it works.

Affiliate advertising is a plan that allows a person or a company, called an associate or a distributor, you obtain a fee from a vendor. At its center, it is a sort of exhibition primarily based totally advertising in addition to some other offers channel on your picture. The associate advances the vendor's object on line through channels like internet-primarily based totally leisure, webweb sites and internet journals, and procures a fee in view of offers of these objects that take place in mild of the development.

In spite of the reality that associates are usually paid a fee for each deal, they are able to likewise be paid for every snap, lead or different type of extrade that their development creates. An associate may be something from a novel blogger raising a logo to an internet site like Groupon, which accomplishes with one-of-a-kind agencies to provide preparations on their objects and administrations.

What Makes Affiliate Marketing Special?
Affiliate advertising is precise in terms of one-of-a-kind forms of advertising — even pressure to be reckoned with advertising. With powerhouse advertising, marks normally pay forces to be reckoned with in advance of an advertising attempt for unique expectations. With associate advertising, associates are paid while an actual extrade happens. Despite the reality that you may install an associate advertising dating with a powerhouse, it is now no longer similar to the same old powerhouse advertising attempt.

A logo's personal internet-primarily based totally leisure advertising likewise contrasts from associate advertising. Affiliates can make use of internet-primarily based totally leisure to increase the logo's object and collect commissions. However, while manufacturers make use of their personal digital leisure channels to increase their objects, they may be raising straightforwardly to consumers, without the inclusion of an outsider.

Likewise, a logo's personal substance advertising contrasts from associate advertising. An associate may want to make use of content material advertising, just like the associate's personal weblog or web website online, to increase the logo's object. Be that because it might also additionally, the logo arrives on the consumer straightforwardly while it advances its object through its web website online or weblog.

The Advantages of Affiliate Marketing
There is a motivation behind why 80% of manufacturers make use of a few types of associate advertising. It works. There are diverse blessings for manufacturers and advertisers who use associate advertising, which includes the following.Affiliate Marketing Advantages For Organizations
Another Productive Deals Channel
Benefits Various Items
Financially savvy
Increment Upper hand
New Crowds Through Powerhouses
Affiliate Advertisers And Admittance To Their Channels
Execution Based Promoting
Information From Affiliates
Investigation and Mission Execution
Simple To Begin And Make due
A few one-of-a-kind blessings are:
More noteworthy Reach
Involving associates for advertising is right here and there like having each an outreach institution and a marketing and marketing company in one. You get a greater noteworthy attain with extra people getting the message out approximately your object. What's greater, the first-rate component of approximately internet-primarily based totally associate advertising is that you may absolutely touch crowds from one facet of the planet to the opopposite.

1.You Pick Who You Need to Work With
Organizations and types may be unique
approximately the associates they determine to
paintings with, making sure that the associate, in
addition to the associate's crowd, notoriety and
content material are stable suits for the object and
the brand.

2. Affiliate Marketing Is Financially savvy
Organizations that use associates simply repay
commissions in the form of adjustments, making
associate advertising a financially savvy method. It
moreover makes it easy to determine associate
charges in keeping with deals.

3. Your Image Gets Affiliate Approval
At the factor while an associate contacts a reliable
crowd, becoming a member of forces with that
associate can circulate that consideration in your
picture. Affiliates that increase your object interior
glad that their crowd reveals vital or enticing can
help with approving your picture and object in
keeping with consumers.

4. Develops Traffic All the greater Rapidly
While associates propose your object through
digital leisure, and their adherents percentage the
ones proposals with companions, their own circle of
relatives and accomplice, it drives increasingly site
visitors in your picture's web website online. What's
greater, it may take place hastily while a survey or a
development clearly takes off.

5. Affiliates Make Designated Content and
Duplicate
Affiliates could make the type of glad and copy this
is usually effective for his or her crowd.
They recognize what works, and it is to their best
benefit to make use of phrases that promote.

Why Use Affiliate Marketing?
Brands and advertisers use associate advertising
as an important evil — some closures. Here are the
main closing targets:

Increment Changes: Affiliate advertising can help
with increasing differences for manufacturers. The
greater people you've got advancing your object,
the greater adjustments, and eventually, offers you
are probably going to have. Selling, all matters
taken into consideration, is and has for all time
been a numbers game.

Develop Brand Mindfulness: Consider associates
logo envoys, spreading interest in your picture
amongst their crowds, who're probably clients of
your object.

Get Information: Utilizing associate advertising may
be an outstanding manner for manufacturers and
advertisers to build up offers statistics that they are
able to then use to determine the locales and types
of clients they want to goal to a more extent.

How Would You Utilize Affiliate Marketing?
For your picture to start with associate advertising, you want to do the legwork for deciding on associates. It's pivotal to do the exam to discover the associates which are fine in shape on your picture and object.

How Really does Affiliate Marketing Work Basically?
At its middle associate advertising is simple, and right here it's miles in six sincere advances:

The associate and the enterprise get right into dating both through an outsider (an associate company) or straightforwardly.
An Affiliate stocks the object and management to their company of decision (typically a connection or a coupon)
Potential consumers are attracted to the connection.
Client lands at the agencies greeting web page
The consumer makes a purchase.
The enterprise receives the offers, and the associate advertiser receives a fee.
Affiliate advertising, in this manner, incorporates 3 (4 at the off hazard which you're the use of a company) companions: The advertiser (likewise known as a distributor), the object supplier (or the person that disperses the objects and the administrations), and the consumer.

The connection among the advertiser and object maker is predicated upon the concept of the preparations installation among them. A consumer will purchase from an enterprise, and the consumer's maximum memorable verbal exchange will accompany the advertiser.

An enterprise can ease out its associate cycle and might not cope with the real interaction, using an associate company, albeit inflated charges are an exciting factor.

A perfect associate advertising attempt is beneficial for every partner. The enterprise and the advertiser acquires profits, and customers get extra person proposals from a confided in source.

Ways to enlist Affiliates
Frequently, your reliable customers will grow to be a part of your fine associates. Search the internet — or make use of a matchmaking device — to discover the bloggers, powerhouses or internet site admins who're as of now advancing your picture or whose concentrations and pastimes line up with the ones of your customers. Investigate the associates your competition is using, and take a look at whether or not they appear OK on your picture.

When you enlist associates in your picture's web website online, you are likewise vulnerable to attract diverse customers who're now active in your picture. While you install a greeting web page in your web website online to sign up associates, make certain it is easy and clean for them to recognise and join. You can likewise make use of packages to paintings together with your associate advertising application, just like the ones supplied through Shopify's utility store.

Affiliate Advancements
Contingent upon your targets and what works fine with associates' crowds, there are numerous approaches for manufacturers to transport closer to associate advertising.

Coupons and boundaries that the associates provide in your picture's objects or administrations are one preference that could feature admirably with clients. Email advertising thru associates is some other preference. Simply take into account in order now no longer to barrage clients with electronic mail advertising through operating with this type of massive quantity of colleagues alongside those lines. A few manufacturers provide motivations, compensating consumers for his or her devotion or references as a sort of associate advertising.

Collaborating with massive media agencies as associates on your picture is one greater preference and one which has been around for a surely lengthy time. It's basically profits sharing and must be feasible with webweb sites, magazines, and tv and radio pronunciations which are to be had to cope with a fee premise.

With the thriving reputation of video and portable, taking part with associates which have extreme regions of power for an on video channels like YouTube and that decorate for flexibility can likewise be crucial in your picture's prosperity.

Step through step commands to Construct an Affiliate Marketing Site

- Choose a Specialty
- Find an associate application the maximum suitable to you
- Facilitating an associate advertising web website online
- Set up subjects and modules
- Create uniqueness specific substance
- Set up analytics
- These are the must-observe movements closer to gather an associate advertising web website online. We must take an in depth gander at them.

1. Choose a Specialty
Since associate advertising may be so aggressive, it's essential to select the proper uniqueness. The proper uniqueness must permit you to specify objects easily, keep away from extra competition and allow you to domesticate a devoted target market.

To start with, we must speak approximately why uniqueness is critical for profitability. Only one out of each ordinary challenge suits referencing objects, and now no longer all objects provide a significant payout for snaps or associate income.

Brandon Gaille of The Blog Millionaire integrated facts on which specialties have been usually worthwhile for bloggers making greater than $2,000 a month. He considered non-public finance because of the maximum worthwhile uniqueness.

At the factor while you paint with one specific logo, you generally do as such through their affiliate application. Each associate application might also additionally have diverse phrases and payouts.

At the factor while you're to start with starting, you should hunt down manufacturers you need to paint with to test whether or not they provide any associate packages. For example, at the off-chance that your web website online is withinside the tour uniqueness, you may need to show it to an associate for a monetary plan flight web website online.

In contrast, associate networks accomplice you with diverse traders, presenting you with a massive quantity of objects to select from.

Amazon Associates is one in all the most important that allows you to earn a fee from any object on Amazon. Similarly, ShareASale is some other large with a 55.7% marketplace percentage that companions with lots of traders from diverse specialties.

2.It's vital to not forget associate fee charges at the same time as selecting your associates.
 Not all associates or object classes are the same. For instance, that is the manner widely Amazon Affiliate's bonus varies through object.

In addition, it is vital to recognize how you are paid at the same time as learning associate packages. Here are the 3 predominant approaches associate packages remember referrals:

Per-click: When a consumer faucets in your connection, the service provider can pay you a small quantity.
Per-lead: You get a small quantity while a consumer faucets in your connection and enters their statistics at the service provider's web website online.
Per-sale: You get a payout while a consumer faucets in your connection and purchases from an affiliated service provider.
3. Facilitating an Affiliate Marketing Site
When you recognize your uniqueness and who you will paint with, now could be the best time to assemble your associate advertising web website online.

To begin with, get a site call. That is the deal that customers will use to navigate to your web website online. For dependable branding and Web optimization, it must be an applicable component in your picked uniqueness.

You'll probably examine that the least hard names withinside the maximum worthwhile specialties are extremely greater steeply-priced or taken altogether, so ensure you do not go along with something unrelated or difficult to recall.

Then, at that factor, you must discover internet facilitating. While your area call resembles the decision quantity for a library ee-e book, the facilitation resembles the shelf the ee-ebook sits on. It's in which all of the files and facts are positioned away associated with your web website online.

Assuming that that looks to be a ton of steps, Bluehost gives each multi functional place, together with a smooth internet clothier, so that you can get your web website online installation in minutes.

4. Set Up Topics and Modules
You should not get over excited in your maximum memorable associate advertising web website online close to appearance. That way you do not have to realize the way to code to assemble an associate advertising web website online that works for you. It's specifically smooth at the off hazard which you make use of an internet clothier for WordPress.

WordPress is a substance control framework (CMS) with many appealing and smooth-to-make use of topics that make making your web website online geared up sincere. In case you do not know which challenge to go along with, HubSpot collected a rundown of the fine topics for associate advertising webweb sites.

When your web website online is installed, modules can assist upload and song your associate joins. An ordinary sort of module for associate entrepreneurs is a connection cloaking module.

Affiliate connections may be a lengthy collection of numbers, which might also additionally reason customers to doubt the connection. Connect cloaking modules like Pretty Connections permit you to to start with direct to a web page beneath neath your URL then the outside associate.

That way joins appear greater dependable and help with balancing the inner and outside connections on every web page. That, thus, assists you with rating better in seek motors.

Create Specialty Explicit Substance
With your web website online installation and geared up to go, all it really is exceeded directly to do is fill it with content material.

Here's in which you will as a substitute now no longer reduce any corners. Effective associates realize superb uniqueness specific substance is critical to getting site visitors in addition to adjustments as properly.

Here are the maximum broadly identified types of content material:

Item surveys and comparisons
The handiest approach to courses and tutorials that function objects and administrations
Reader testimonials
Instruments or administrations roundups
Along with those provides deliberate on function diverse associate joins, you may compose on quite plenty any supportive factor, interior your uniqueness and upload a connection or to affiliated objects.

To brainstorm best substance thoughts on your web website online, contemplate what your target target market maximum regularly searches for on the internet. At the end of the day, perform a little catchphrase studies.

You should not position assets into a sturdy software program at this time. There are a variety of loose watchword studies gadgets to help you with locating topics with wonderful seek extent that are not excessively cutthroat on your new web website online.

Online discussions like Quora additionally deliver treasured know-how into the inquiries and problems people regularly have on your uniqueness. On the off chance that you run a non-public finance weblog and look for a vast challenge like "credit" and channel through questions, you will sing down a variety of appropriate factors really well worth developing a put up round.

Set Up Analytics
You might not begin raking in that body of thoughts after studying the way to gather your associate advertising web website online. Chances are, some matters will resonate together with your target market at the same time as others will now no longer.

The vital component is to recognize which paintings and why, so that you can mirror them.

Here are the 2 maximum vital measurements to measure:

Clicks: This helps you to realize how regularly your visitors interact together along with your connections — and which connections play out the fine. To song clicks, you should use one or the opposite installation of your Google Analytics to song joins using specialized code or make use of a module like MonsterInsights.
Earnings Per Snap (EPC): This is your income separated through the whole quantity of snaps. It can help you realize which associate companions your target market will buy the maximum and which connection positions are the fine. From that factor, you may recognize the connections that go back the maximum benefit.
Final Contemplations: How To Assemble an Affiliate Marketing Site in 6 Stages
For amateurs, building an associate advertising web website online requires making plans and studies to ensure you are choosing the proper uniqueness for you.

From that factor, the principal part of constructing an associate web website online is developing a treasured substance and monitoring your outcomes. With sufficient endurance and interest in the method, you are sure to efficiently adapt your weblog.

On the off-chance that you're geared up to get the whole thing rolling with associate advertising, install your web website online with an instinctive, smooth-to-make use of devices like Bluehost's Web clothier today.

Eight Affiliate Marketing Skills Every Successful Affiliate Needs.

Nowadays, associate advertising is in excessive demand to make coins on the internet. Affiliate advertising is likewise taken into consideration as performance-primarily based totally advertising that offers a possible manner for the traders. Initially, you need to marketplace the internet-primarily based totally objects to the customers, at the off-chance that a person purchases the objects primarily based totally on principal regions of power for you, you may get a fee from the company. Individuals must have specific skills to be successful withinside the associate advertising subject.

If you need to earn greater coins thru internet primarily based totally advertising, you must be specialized in several regions. You must have a functionality to create commercials inside the web sites, manipulate your crew and coins, and cap potential to attend to extra problems in a regular progression. A massive part of the companies, promote their objects in a wonderful manner with the help of associate marketer. Let see the skills required for associate advertising for every powerful associate desires:

1. Information In Web composition:
In fashion, the internet composition calls for a greater variety of skills. Individuals should examine

many thoughts to show right into a first rate internet site expert due to the fact it's miles loaded up with plenty of plan selections and complex coding languages. In any case, nowadays, the internet site structure is considered as a less difficult one while in comparison with one-of-a-kind skills.

The more a part of the internet facilitating locations provides loose smooth to apply internet designers with smooth drag and drop templates. Initially, you must have a simple statistics approximately the plans and PC skills to get development on this subject.

2. Critical questioning And Critical questioning skills:
Critical questioning and crucial questioning skills are taken into consideration because of the critical knowledge for associate entrepreneurs. On the off-chance that you have a wonderful crucial questioning knowledge, you may be capable of as it should gauge your advertising method. At the same time, you may get a concept to similarly expand your skills in which you're missing in associate advertising. Because the associate entrepreneurs are autonomous, they should select the proper solution for looking after their approaching problems.

Direction is taken into consideration as a crucial aspect for the advertising subject due to the fact a massive part of people depend upon their stoop to make a proper preference. You have plenty of gadgets to manufacture your insight.

3. Ought to Have A Technical Expertise: Nowadays, associate advertising is in excessive demand to make coins on the internet. Affiliate advertising is likewise taken into consideration as performance-primarily based totally advertising that offers a a hit manner for the traders. Initially, you need to marketplace the internet-primarily based totally objects to the customers, withinside the occasion that a person purchases the objects primarily based totally on regions of power for you, you may get a fee from the company. Individuals must have specific skills to be successful withinside the associate advertising subject.

To earn greater coins thru internet primarily based totally advertising, you must be specialized in several regions. You must have a functionality to create commercials inside the web sites, manipulate your crew and coins, and cap potential to attend to extra problems in a regular progression. A massive part of the companies, promote their objects in a wonderful manner with the help of associate marketer. Let see the skills required for associate advertising for every fruitful associate desires:

1. Information In Web structure:

Information In Web structure

In fashion, the internet structure calls for a greater variety of skills. Individuals should examine many thoughts to show right into a first rate internet site expert due to the fact it's miles loaded up with plenty of plan selections and complex coding languages. By and through, nowadays, the internet site structure is considered as a less difficult one while in comparison with one-of-a-kind skills.

The considerable majority of the internet facilitating locations provide loose smooth to recognize internet designers with smooth drag and drop templates. Initially, you must have a simple statistics approximately the plans and PC skills to get final results on this subject.

2. Critical questioning And Thinking skills:

Critical questioning and questioning skills are taken into consideration because of the critical knowledge for associate entrepreneurs. On the off-chance that you have a wonderful crucial questioning knowledge, you may be capable of as it should gauge your advertising method. At the same time, you may get a concept to similarly expand your skills in which you're missing in associate advertising. Because the associate entrepreneurs are as autonomous, they should select the proper solution for looking after their approaching problems.

Independent route is taken into consideration as a crucial aspect for the advertising subject due to the fact that the bulk of people depend upon their stoop to make a proper preference. You have plenty of devices to manufacture your insight.

3. Ought to Have A Technical Expertise:
Ought to Have A Technical Expertise If you need to show into an associate marketer, you must have simple technical statistics in advertising. You should discover ways to create touchdown pages, cap potential to cope with diverse problems and install your tracker. These are all of the base technical statistics you must have.

4. Creativity Ability:
If you need to show right into a fruitful associate marketer, the innovative knowledge is the principle key aspect. The majority of the fruitful entrepreneurs create progressive advertising techniques and campaigns, deliver appealing substance to their customers and the cap potential to foster tremendous logo characters. The creativity knowledge can not be trained through anyone, it must comprise your non-public vision. On the occasion when you are wonderful in innovative knowledge, associate advertising is the proper platform for your destiny.

5. Data Analytic Expertise:
Data Analytic Ability
Data evaluation is taken into consideration as some other wonderful-sounding set knowledge. As an advertising advertiser, you'll be sincerely looking in order that facts may want to see your advertising campaign's destiny paintings. As properly as, the analytics may be applied to parent out the forms of customers you're attracting while the customers visited your web website online ultimately and some other substance works. A part of the analytical gadgets can deliver final results in visible codecs like lovely graphs.

6. Ought to Have Communication Expertise:
Communication is a wonderful manner to provide your associate objects to customers. You must have the cap potential to give an explanation for the blessings of the objects you're going to sale. You actually need to keep an easy date together with your customers and try to interface on a non-public stage with them. As an associate marketer, you need to similarly expand your consumer lives through presenting wonderful objects and administrations. The fine associate entrepreneurs create regions of power for a with their customers.

7. Leadership Ability:

The entrepreneurs must have a management best to manipulate the crew people. Building a crew is one of the difficult responsibilities for the associate entrepreneurs; you must have a specialized knowledge to direct them in the precise manner. You should assign the responsibilities on your teams, teach the representatives, geared up to stand the problems and maintain them motivated.

eight. Marketing And Sales Abilities:
For promoting a selected object, the associate entrepreneurs must have advertising and income knowledge. As a marketer, you need to create site visitors on your manufacturers and objects. The considerable majority of people buy an object which has excessive site visitors. You must have the cap potential to give an explanation for the blessings remembered for the object and appeal to the customers to buy. Attempt to examine as many stuff in advertising as you may.

In this manner, those are all of the vital skills required for associate entrepreneurs. Make usage of these statistics to be successful withinside the associate advertising subject.